WHEN SOMEONE YOU LOVE IS ADDICTED

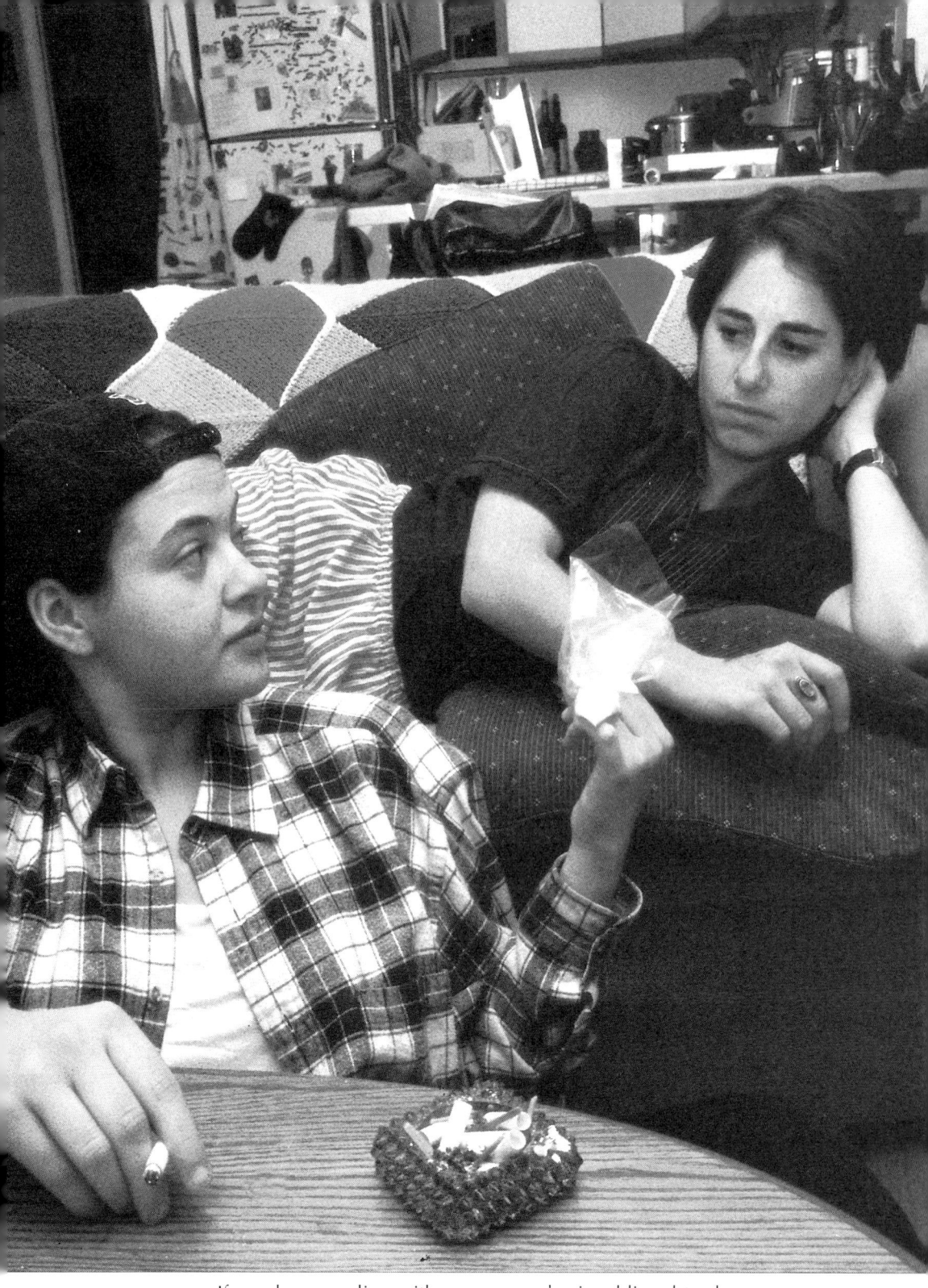

If you know or live with someone who is addicted to drugs or alcohol, you are not alone. Most people face this situation at some point in their lives.

THE DRUG ABUSE PREVENTION LIBRARY

WHEN SOMEONE YOU LOVE IS ADDICTED

by Jessica Hanan

THE ROSEN PUBLISHING GROUP, INC.
NEW YORK

For Lance Krubner—nagging works!

I would like to thank the following people for their help and encouragement: my daughters, Madelynn Lund and Victoria Hanan; Michael Alexandersen; Peter Deksnis; Lance Krubner; and my editor, Michele Drohan.

The people pictured in this book are only models. They in no way practice or endorse the activities illustrated. Captions serve only to explain the subjects of photographs and do not in any way imply a connection between the real-life models and the staged situations.

Published in 1999 by The Rosen Publishing Group, Inc.
29 East 21st Street, New York, NY 10010

Copyright © 1999 by The Rosen Publishing Group, Inc.

First Edition

All rights reserved. No part of this book may be reproduced in any form without permission in writing from the publisher, except by a reviewer.

Library of Congress Cataloging-in-Publication Data
Hanan, Jessica.
　　When someone you love is addicted / by Jessica Hanan.
　　　　p.　　cm.— (The Drug abuse prevention library)
　　Includes bibliographical references and index.
　　Summary: Discusses how and why people may become addicted to drugs or alcohol, the effects such addictions can have on family members and friends, and ways to get help.
　　ISBN 0-8239-2831-4
　　1. Drug Abuse—Juvenile literature. 2. Alcoholism—Juvenile literature. 3. Narcotic addicts—Family relationships—Juvenile literature. 4. Alcoholics—Family relationships—Juvenile literature. [1. Alcoholism. 2. Drug abuse. 3. Addicts—Family relationships.] I. Title.　II. Series.
HV5809.5.H35　1998
362.29'13—dc21　　　　　　　　　　　　　　　　　　　　92-39622
　　　　　　　　　　　　　　　　　　　　　　　　　　　　　CIP
　　　　　　　　　　　　　　　　　　　　　　　　　　　　　AC

Manufactured in the United States of America

Contents

	Introduction 6
Chapter 1	Addiction: How and Why? 9
Chapter 2	The Effects of Addiction 22
Chapter 3	How You Are Affected by a Loved One's Addiction 32
Chapter 4	When and How You Can Help 41
Chapter 5	What the Future Holds 51
	Glossary 58
	Where to Go for Help 60
	For Further Reading 62
	Index 63

Introduction

The door slammed. In his room, Jamal could hear his parents fighting. He turned up his stereo, but he could still hear them screaming.

Dad was drunk again. Jamal heard the names his parents yelled at each other. He could imagine the scene going on downstairs.

Jamal felt trapped. He wanted to help his mom but knew that he would have to face his father the moment he set foot into the kitchen. So Jamal stayed in his room and hid. He took a pillow and covered his head. Jamal tried to block out his shame, guilt, fear, and pain, but nothing helped.

Jamal lay in bed shaking and thinking, Why is this happening?

If you are reading this book, it is most likely because you know someone struggling with drug or alcohol addiction. You are not alone. Many of your neighbors, friends, family members, and teachers may know or live with someone who is addicted to drugs or alcohol. This person could be a parent, a sibling, or a friend. People in your situation are facing many of the same problems. This book will help you cope with the many issues surrounding addiction.

First it will help you understand addiction. You will learn how and why it happens, and how addiction affects your loved one. You'll also see how addiction affects you and your life. You may be feeling confused, guilty, angry, and ashamed. This book will help you deal with these painful emotions.

You also will read about ways to help your loved one and what you should or should not do for him or her. And you'll see how Tough Love, intervention, and codependency can help or hurt your situation.

This book addresses the recovery process and explains what your loved one must deal with during this time period. You may be asking, "What if help is refused?" or "What if there's a relapse?" This book will deal with those tough questions as well.

The most important thing to remember is that the addiction is not your fault. You are not the cause of the problem and you are not responsible for fixing it. This book provides you with the information you need to help your loved one and yourself.

Television stimulates our senses and creates cravings. Most people are able to resist their cravings, but when people are addicted to drugs, they have no control over them.

CHAPTER 1

Addiction: How and Why?

You are watching television. You feel relaxed and comfortable. Then the program breaks and a commercial begins. Thick gooey chocolate sauce runs down fresh vanilla ice cream. Suddenly you swallow. You can almost taste the cool, sweet cream. You wonder, Is there ice cream in the freezer? Should you leave the comfort of your chair to check?

You have suddenly developed a craving! For you, this sudden desire is controllable. You stay in your chair; the show returns. As you become absorbed in the show, that yearning for ice cream vanishes.

Most people are able to control cravings. However, when someone is addicted to a drug, it's not that easy. When a chemical is present, the urge for the substance does not disappear. Instead, the longing for it increases. Nothing—except taking that substance—can make the craving go away.

Some experts believe people can become addicted to a behavior, such as shopping, gambling, or exercising. They feel that their desire to perform these actions can be as intense as the urge for some to drink or use drugs. The focus of this book, however, is drug and alcohol addiction.

Addiction is an overpowering urge to continue the use of one or more chemical substances. An addicted person can't stop using these substances without experiencing painful withdrawal symptoms. An addiction overcomes common sense. A person will continue to use a substance despite all of its harmful effects. Drug and/or alcohol use continues in spite of illness, job loss, debt, or pain caused to a loved one. The chemical substance becomes the only concern.

How Does Addiction Happen?

Addiction usually does not occur overnight. While some people become addicted after using a drug once, for most people it happens gradually. It usually starts with experimentation, then moves on to regular use. Soon the person arranges his or her life around drug use, and finally develops an addiction.

As soon as Stacey got to the party, someone handed her a beer. She'd never had one before, but she drank it quickly. Weaving slightly, she walked to the fridge for another. Stacey thought, What's the big deal? I feel pretty good. Drinking the second can of beer made her feel giddy and relaxed. Wow, she thought, this is fun!

Stacey tried the beer out of curiosity. Like many people, Stacey didn't believe trying drugs and/or alcohol could create problems. People tend to think experimenting with drugs is safe. For some people this may be the case, but in other instances experimentation with drugs or alcohol continues. Then the person may begin trying other substances or start using the one particular drug more often. Using and experimenting with different drugs and/or alcohol is the first step toward addiction.

In the next stage of addiction the person believes he or she must use drugs or alcohol to have fun. The person relies on the drug to feel good. During this stage it may be hard to recognize any changes in the person's attitude or behavior.

When people's lives and activities revolve around drugs and alcohol, they have crossed the line into abuse.

Soon Stacey was drinking with her friends every weekend at parties. She thought drinking had improved her social life. After a few beers, Stacey felt more comfortable at these parties. She met new people and did not feel self-conscious or unsure of herself. Drinking had become a regular feature in her life. She no longer thought about drinking; it had become a normal weekend activity. Stacey was becoming more popular, and she was still doing well in school. Stacey felt she had it all.

A person passes into the next stage of addiction when drug or alcohol use becomes the focus of his or her life. The drug abuser now has a new circle of friends, most of whom use drugs, too. A person in this stage is usually using many different types of drugs. This is because he or she has developed a tolerance. Tolerance is when a person needs more and more of a drug to get the original effect. And a person will often use different drugs when he or she has developed a tolerance for one. This person may start to steal, violate the trust of family and friends, or have trouble at work or school. Often appearance and personality are also changing.

Full addiction occurs when the person must use drugs in order to feel normal. Using drugs is no longer fun or pleasurable, but is required in order to function. This happens because drug and alcohol addiction affects the brain, causing it to function differently. The brain doesn't work the way it used to. That's why an addicted person will continue to use drugs despite all the terrible things that happen to him or her.

Why Does Addiction Happen?
Except for infants born to addicted mothers, people are not born addicted. Many people drink or try different drugs. Most of these people experience some type of high. But not all of those people become addicted. Why?

Several possible influences have been stated by different experts. These influences were published by the National Institute of Drug Abuse (NIDA). Some include:

- friends who use drugs
- lack of willpower
- drugs in a person's environment
- a parent's behavior
- a person's financial situation
- mental illness
- childhood experiences
- a problem personality
- inherited tendency toward addiction

Half-awake, Will got out of bed and immediately fell on his face. He had left his books piled in front of his bed. Picking himself up, Will moaned, "What else will go wrong today?"

Like Will, little mishaps can set the mood for the rest of your day. Similarly, your life is affected by several factors, such as where you live, your school, the weather, your family, or the amount of money your parents earn.

Your behavior and character are shaped by all or some of these conditions. They are small samples of the situations affecting your life. Likewise, there is no one reason why a

Living on the streets makes a person more vulnerable to the dangers of drug addiction.

person becomes addicted. Addiction is caused by many complex conditions and issues that occur in a person's life.

Addictive Personality?

When your body's ability to ward off diseases has been decreased, you become more prone to disease. Some people can go with less sleep than others, some can have a poor diet and still be healthy, and some need to get their full eight hours and three balanced meals a day to remain healthy. A person's susceptibility depends on a variety of factors, which may be biological, environmental, emotional, or physical. The same philosophy exists when it comes to drug and alcohol addiction.

So, is there such a thing as an addictive personality? The scientific community has not come to a definite conclusion on this issue. Experts think some people have personalities predisposed to their becoming addicted. There are many factors that may influence this predisposition. People with these high-risk factors are believed to have an addictive personality. These factors can include some or all of the following:

- one or two family members that are chemically dependent, such as parents, grandparents, or siblings
- feelings of stress
- fear of failure
- few interests or activities
- need or desire to avoid problems
- not caring about oneself

Another idea about addictive personality is that the personality develops because of (or after) the addiction. Experts explain that the addiction causes a second type of personality. This personality is driven by the addiction; it is responsible for the addicted person's unhealthy, unkind, dangerous, and immoral behavior. This addictive personality takes over your loved one and covers up his or her true personality.

Why Does Someone Turn to Drugs?

Her head throbbing, Lynn left the school building. She noticed how the other students whispered as she walked past. Lynn worried about what they thought of her. She was troubled about her schoolwork and her parents' money problems. Thinking about these problems made her headache worse.

Lynn could smell the weed as she entered Mary's house. Flopping into a chair, Lynn accepted the blunt and took a long hit. Exhaling slowly, she felt her headache start to disappear. Her mind was empty. No thoughts. No worries. Finally Lynn felt calm, happy, and relaxed.

Life is full of ups and downs. Everyone has had a bad day at one time or another. Some have more than others. Difficult times can bring pain, disappointment, stress, worries, and overwhelming pressure. People handle their problems differently. One person may play music. Another person may confide in a friend. Another may go for a walk. All these are healthy ways to handle life's stresses. But sometimes people seek out destructive ways to deal with problems. They abuse drugs and alcohol as a temporary escape. And they like the high they feel when they use drugs. While everyone's goal is to feel happy, addiction can develop when people consistently use drugs to deal with problems.

Jim had a big game. As star quarterback, everyone expected him to perform. Game time was approaching. Jim opened his locker to change into his uniform. He reached for the bottle and took a quick drink. The alcohol stung the inside of his mouth. He took several more swallows. The "buzz" he was feeling boosted his morale. Now he knew he could perform. Now he would do well.

Some people feel they must be perfect. They may have parents with unreasonably high expectations. They may play under coaches who demand perfect performances. Or they may have teachers who judge them harshly and unfairly.

The need to perform well, please others, impress classmates, or be the perfect child can cause an unbearable burden. Such pressures may cause people to turn to drugs and/or alcohol.

There are several other reasons why someone may turn to drugs. They include:

- **Boredom.** Life's constant routine may not be interesting enough. Drugs may add a new dimension, a change.

- **Peer pressure**. At a party all your friends are using drugs. They keep offering you drugs until, finally, you use the drug, too.

- **Excitement**. Some people enjoy living on the edge—being dangerous and taking chances. Using drugs and alcohol adds an element of risk.

- **Rebellion.** Everyone says, "Don't do drugs!" Sometimes the fact that you are told no becomes reason enough.

- **Imitation.** Role models are important to everyone. All people identify with someone: a big brother or sister, a parent, a movie star, or a musician. If a role model uses drugs or alcohol, you may be influenced to imitate his or her behavior.

No matter why a person turns to drugs, drug addiction comes about gradually. Experimenting with drugs or alcohol does not always cause addiction. A few people decide they have explored enough, and do not use the drug again. Others can use alcohol in a responsible manner, which is legal for people over twenty-one years old,

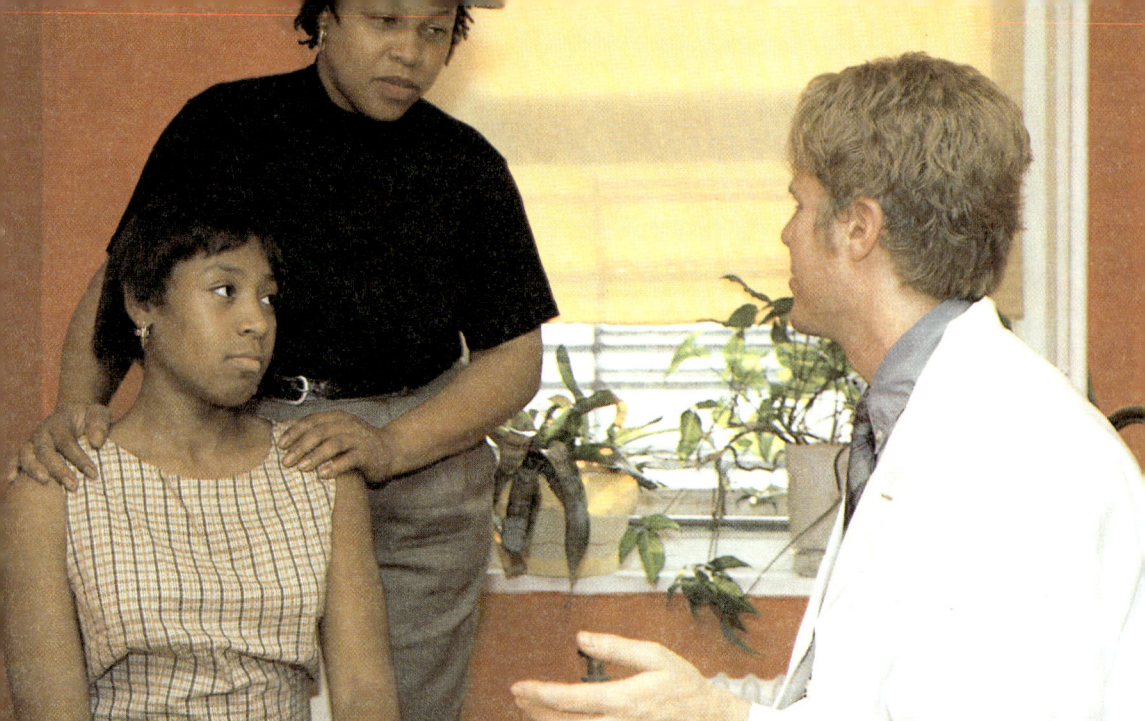

When a person has a drug or alcohol problem, the best thing to do is reach out and get professional help.

and not have a problem with it. However, the effects from drugs and alcohol vary from person to person. There are no rules that help people know how they will be affected when they start using. Nobody plans to become addicted to drugs. But when it happens, it has devastating effects to a person's life.

Addiction Is an Illness

Even though many people are affected by drug and alcohol addiction, it has often been looked at in a negative and unsympathetic light. People once saw addiction as a moral problem or a lack of willpower. But doctors and scientists have recognized drug and alcohol addiction as a disease, a chronic illness like diabetes. And so people who are addicted should not be blamed for their illness. But addicted people can and should be responsible for their recovery. Your loved one can get treatment. But recovery is a lifelong treatment. Without treatment a person can die.

CHAPTER 2

The Effects of Addiction

*P*eople addicted to drugs or alcohol suffer both psychologically and physically. Those suffering from a psychological addiction think they need the drug in order to function. When a person is suffering from a physical addiction, his or her body needs the drug in order to function and will suffer from withdrawal symptoms without it.

Psychological Effects

The psychological effects of drug use may exist in all or one of the following forms: isolation, depression, guilt, shame, and denial.

Drug addiction structures the addicted person's life. Most activities the person performs become driven by his or her drug

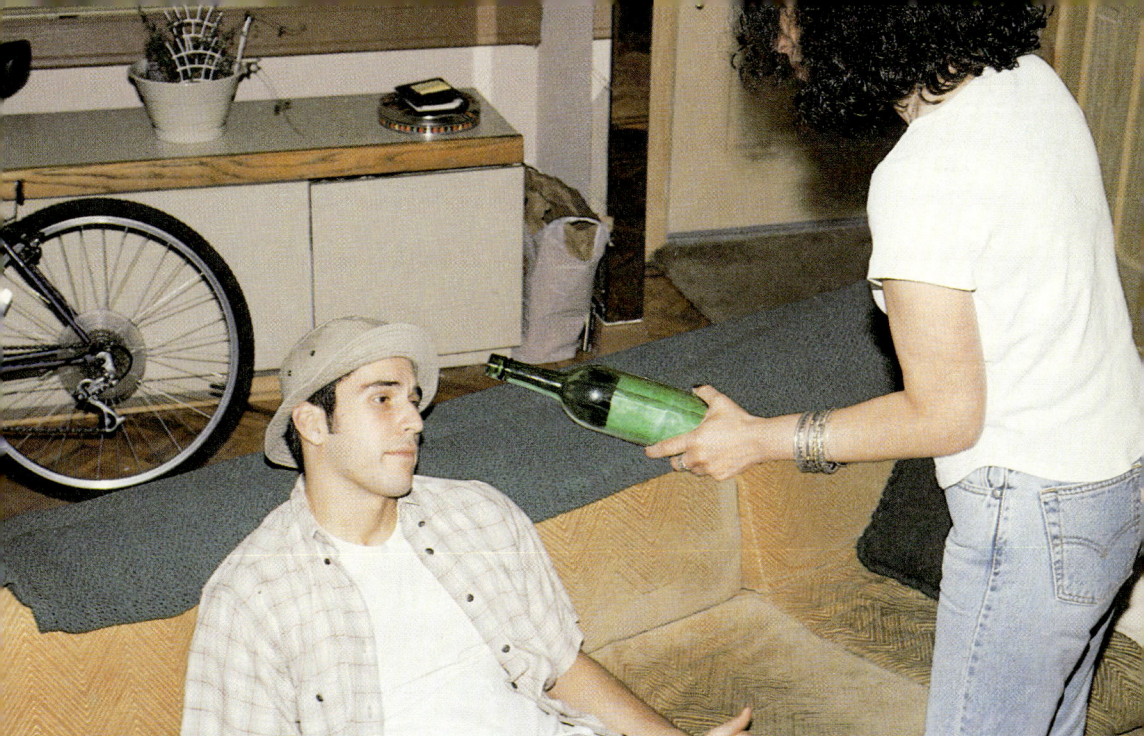

Addiction is such a severe illness that a person will deny the problem, despite direct confrontation by family and friends.

abuse. These activities may include lying, stealing, or acting violent toward a loved one. When drug addicts become aware of these actions they become guilt stricken and filled with shame. But their addiction overcomes common sense and compassion.

In order to deal with feelings of guilt, people addicted to drugs will deny that they have a problem. Denial is when people seem unaware of or refuse to admit the amount of or how frequently they use a drug. They don't believe that their drug addiction causes any problems. Their feelings of shame are relieved by denial.

As young children Ken and his brother, Rob, were always close. They were also practi-

cal jokers—each always trying to out-trick the other. As teens, their horsing around was rough but always friendly.

But lately Ken has noticed changes in Rob's behavior. Often Rob comes home and locks himself in his room. He stays there for hours. When he's not in his room, Rob seems distant. Ken can't figure out what's wrong. He can see Rob changing but doesn't know why.

Yesterday Ken saw Rob horsing around with his friends in school. Then later, when Ken passed Rob in the hallway, his brother looked his way, waved, and smiled. Suddenly Ken thought the "old" Rob had returned.

After school Ken got home first. As Rob walked through the door Ken jumped in front, blocking Rob's path. It was a childish prank but one they always used to play. But today was different.

Shoving Ken out of his way, Rob started cursing in a loud, nasty tone. When Rob finally stopped yelling, he marched up to his room and slammed the door.

Ken sat on the floor feeling shocked and bewildered. A few hours ago, Rob had been happy and friendly. Now he was cruel and abrupt. What's gotten into him? Ken thought.

Addiction causes a person to behave differently. These changes occur slowly. Behavioral

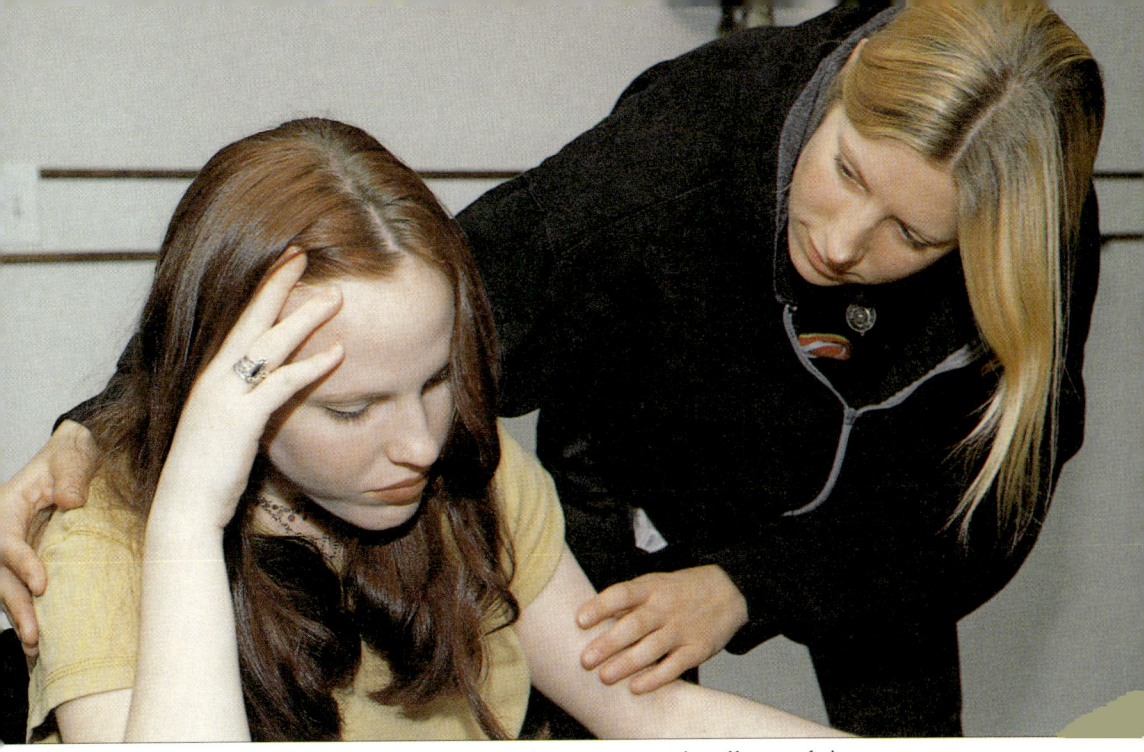

Depression is one of the many devastating side effects of drug addiction.

changes are another psychological effect of drug abuse. You may notice several differences in the way your loved one behaves. Severe mood swings are an example. At times, the person may be kind, giving, and friendly. Then suddenly he or she becomes anxious, angry, violent, and depressed.

Sally and Larry had known each other since grade school. When she moved away they kept in touch. Her mother was constantly complaining about the phone bill. But in the last few weeks Larry never took Sally's phone calls. His mother kept giving Sally one excuse after another. But Larry didn't return her calls, either. Sally didn't understand what was happening. One day Sally and her Mom went back to the old neighborhood. While her Mom shopped, Sally decided to go to the park. As she walked around, she spotted Larry. He was hanging out with some creepy-looking people. Larry didn't look like himself, either. He looked thin and sick. Waving and shouting hello, Sally started to walk toward him, but Larry pretended that he didn't even know her.

Someone addicted to drugs may isolate him- or herself from friends and family. Old friends suddenly seem like enemies because the addiction has changed the addict's personality. A drug addict may lose touch with reality and not be able to recognize right from wrong. He or she has difficulty understanding the consequences of his or her actions. Certain drugs may cause your loved one to feel like a different person—someone who is indestructible. These feelings can put a person in some dangerous and/or violent situations.

The Physical Effects of Addiction

Once a person becomes addicted to a chemical substance, the most immediate general physical effect is withdrawal. Drug or alcohol addiction often includes physical dependence on the substance. When the presence of the substance suddenly

Addiction makes a person physically ill. Withdrawal symptoms can be especially painful.

decreases, the person's body lets him or her know that more is required. If these warnings are ignored, the body reacts violently. Withdrawal is characterized by vomiting, sweating, trembling, and convulsions (abnormal contractions of the muscles).

There are many physical effects of drug abuse. They vary, depending on the drug, the person, and the length of time the drug has been used.

Drugs that are commonly abused fall into four main categories: depressants, hallucinogens, narcotics, and stimulants.

Depressants

Alcohol—The most commonly abused substance. Effects of abuse include slurred speech, distorted vision and hearing, poor judgment, poor coordination, liver disease, blackouts, brain damage, violent behavior, and severe withdrawal symptoms.

Tranquilizers—The most common are phenobarbital, Valium, and Seconal. Common street names include downers, sleeping pills, reds, and rainbows. Effects of abuse include slurred speech, impaired judgment, disorientation, slower breathing and heart rate, loss of appetite, drowsiness, poor coordination, severe withdrawal symptoms, and death from an overdose.

Hallucinogens

Marijuana—Often referred to as weed, pot, a joint, or a blunt. Common side effects include sleepiness, poor memory, reduced coordination, bloodshot eyes, decreased inhibitions, increased appetite, mood swings, lung disease, and difficulty learning.

PCP (phencyclidine)—Most common street names are angel dust and powder. Hazards of use include extreme anxiety or depression, poor memory, perceptual difficulties, aggressiveness, increased heart rate, decrease in muscle coordination, muddled speech, decreased ability to feel pain, convulsions, and death from overdose.

LSD (lysergic acid diethylamine)—On the street it is known as acid and trips. The effects of use are extreme anxiety or depression, perceptual difficulties, aggressiveness, increased heart rate, sleeplessness, decrease in muscle coordination, mood swings, emotional breakdowns, flashbacks, and permanent brain damage.

Inhalants—They can be gasoline, glue, laughing gas, and whippits. The effects of use are severe mood swings, nervous system damage, poor vision and memory, dizziness, headaches, muscle weakness, irregular heartbeat, tiredness, nausea, liver and brain damage, and sudden death.

Narcotics

Some narcotics are used in the medical field to provide pain relief. Commonly abused narcotics include Darvon, codeine, heroin, morphine, and Percodan. On the street these drugs may be called smack, China white, and junk. Abuse of narcotics can result in drowsiness, slurred speech, narrowed pupils, slowed respiration, nausea, tremors, slowed heart rate, coma, and death from overdose.

Stimulants

Cocaine—On the street cocaine can be

Part of recovering from addiction is avoiding the familiar places where a person bought or used drugs.

referred to as coke, crack, and blow. The hazards of abuse include enlarged pupils, violent behavior, anxiety, paranoia, damage to nasal passages, increased heart rate and breathing, heart attacks, seizures, breathing problems, reduced ability to fight infections, and death from overdose.

Amphetamines and Methamphetamine—Amphetamines include Benzedrine and Dexedrine. Common street names are speed, uppers, and crystal. Common effects of amphetamine abuse are enlarged pupils, irregular heart rate, sleeplessness, increased physical activity, problems breathing, paranoia, loss of touch with reality, brain damage, hallucinations, convulsions, and death from an overdose.

Physical addiction can be overcome with treatment. When an addicted person successfully beats the physical addiction, he or she no longer experiences withdrawal symptoms. The person no longer physically craves the drug. But psychological addiction is different. The psychological craving may never go away. That is why recovery is a lifelong treatment. Recovering from an addiction is a long, hard journey. But many people do recover when they are committed to fighting the disease and staying well. There are many different types of treatment, and each addicted person will recover in his or her own way. Finding the right treatment, and sticking with it, is essential for the addicted person to take back control over his or her life.

CHAPTER 3

How You Are Affected by a Loved One's Addiction

That morning, Jen had asked her brother for a ride home from the movies for herself and her friends—he had promised her he would be there.

As Jen and her friends left the movie theater, she looked up and down the street for him. Checking her watch, she turned to her friends and told them her brother would be there soon.

Fifteen minutes passed. She left her friends and went to call home but no one answered. Returning, Jen told her friends he must be on his way. After another ten minutes, Jen's friends started complaining. Finally one of them called her mother and had her bring them all home. Jen felt embarrassed, hurt, and depressed.

When she arrived home her mood changed. As Jen entered the house she smelled the weed. Now she knew why her brother had never shown up. Jen was furious and disgusted. He had promised! Why wasn't his promise to her more important than smoking dope?

Like Jen, some of you may have experienced being disappointed and hurt by someone you love. It's natural to have these experiences in your relationships with family and friends. But when these situations occur because of your loved one's drug and alcohol abuse, it can be especially difficult. Remember that feeling disappointed and hurt is not uncommon and that it's not your fault that this is happening.

Changing Moods and Stress

Everyone has experienced changes in moods. At one time or another most people have experienced happiness, sadness, guilt, depression, jealousy, or disgust. Emotions are a normal part of life. But when a loved one is addicted you may experience more than your share. Anger and hate may become shame and guilt; happiness may turn into confusion and disgust. You are riding on an emotional roller-coaster. Dealing with these constantly changing emotions results in a lot of stress and tension.

Stress can have some very negative effects on people. It can affect them both

The stress of dealing with a loved one struggling with addiction can make your life feel like an emotional roller-coaster.

physically and psychologically. People affected by stress may tire easily, sleep poorly, or be prone to colds and the flu. Too much stress can also lead to behavioral problems such as being loud, rude, and disrespectful; cutting classes or ditching school; and being quiet and withdrawn. All of these are symptoms of the effect your loved one's addiction may have on you.

Added Responsibility and Abuse

A loved one's addiction may cause you to have additional responsibilities, too. Did you ever clean up after a drunk sister or brother? Do you help care for your younger siblings when your mom is passed out on the couch? Have you had to cover up when a parent, sibling, or friend was too "wasted" to go to work? All of these are examples of situations you should not have to face. You are not responsible for the actions or behavior that result from the addiction of your loved one.

Eric's mom was screaming at him. She told him he was lazy, stupid, and worthless. The nasty words poured out of her mouth, until finally she staggered out of his room. Eric just sat there and shook. What else could he do?

Eric felt worthless. His mom's words were still ringing in his ears as he started to think, Maybe she's right.

People who are addicted to drugs may be abusive to others. There are three kinds of abusive behavior: verbal, physical, and sexual. And they all have devastating effects. In Eric's case, his mom is verbally abusive. Its effect on Eric is destroying his self-worth and causing him great emotional pain. The physical and emotional pain experienced by any form of abusive behavior can cause major problems in a person's life.

If you are experiencing abuse from an addicted parent, sibling, or friend, remember you are not to blame. Your loved one is suffering from an illness and

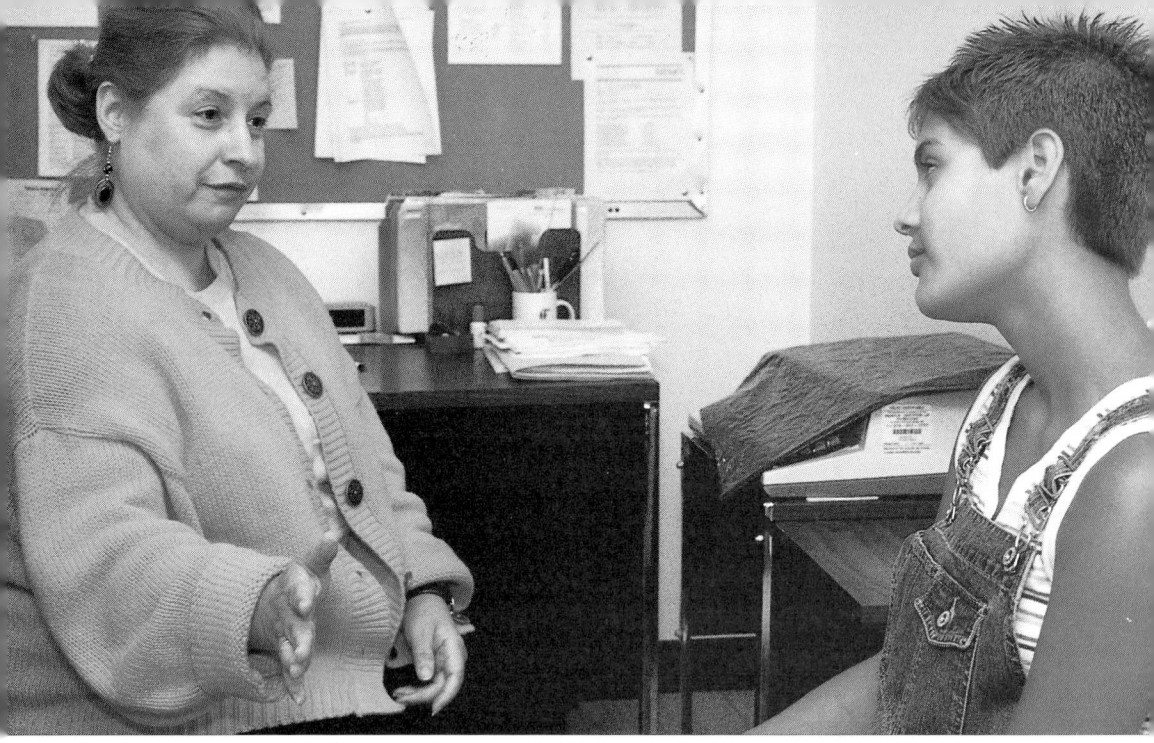

By talking with a trusted adult, you will be able to express your emotions in a healthy way and get help for your loved one.

needs help. It is the addiction that is responsible, and only your loved one can do anything about it. However, if you are being physically or sexually abused you should seek help right away. You may want to tell a trusted adult, such as a relative, a teacher, or a religious leader. If you are in immediate danger, see if you can move in with a relative or close friend's family. Then, with their aid, seek help for yourself and your loved one.

Codependency

The doorbell rang. When Lisa opened the door, Maggie, her best friend, practically fell on top of her. Lisa led Maggie to her bedroom, eased Maggie onto the bed, and went to the phone. When Maggie's mom answered, Lisa told her that Maggie had stayed after school for help with math and would be home late.

Lisa knew all about Maggie's drug problem and, as usual, was covering for Maggie, who was high.

Maggie is off the hook. She will not have to suffer the consequences of arriving home late or deal with her mom's discovering her drug problem. By covering up Maggie's actions, Lisa is helping Maggie to continue her addiction. Without realizing it, Lisa is an enabler.

An enabler tries to control, disguise, or excuse the loved one's addictive behavior. Anyone in a relationship with someone who is chemically dependent is affected by the loved one's condition. These individuals often become codependent. If you are codependent you may feel responsible for your loved one's drug abuse. Sometimes you may even deny that there is a problem. You may be easily manipulated by the addicted person. He or she will know exactly what to say to get you to do something to help him or her.

If you are codependent, you may feel a need to control the addicted person's behavior. You may feel that if you were perfect, your loved one would not be a drug

Support groups are places where people share experiences in a safe and confidential atmosphere.

abuser. Sometimes you may judge yourself too harshly, you may be too critical of yourself, and you may not stand up for yourself. Codependency may cause you to take on too much responsibility or follow another's wishes rather than your own.

Codependency is a condition that develops as a result of your loved one's addiction. It can have devastating effects on your life. If you are codependent you might not want to share your problems. You may feel no one else understands or knows what you are experiencing. But that's not true; there are several groups made up of individuals in similar situations. There are support groups, such as Al-Anon or Nar-Anon, that can provide help and understanding to you.

Can Addiction Happen to Me?

You may be asking yourself this question. You read about the causes of addiction, how it starts, and how it affects the body. You probably remember reading that a person's friends, family, and neighborhood may influence how that person could be affected by drugs and alcohol. And that the possibility of becoming addicted to drugs or alcohol may be inherited. But does that mean you will become addicted?

No. Even if you have a family member who has become addicted to drugs or alcohol, it doesn't mean that you will have problems with drugs. You may be at a higher risk to addiction if you use them. But you can make smart choices in your life to avoid the dangers of addiction.

The fact that you are reading this book is one indication that you know how to choose wisely. By making friends who stay drug free and exploring positive activities, you can protect yourself against the dangers of addiction. By expressing your feelings and dealing with stress in a healthy way, you can avoid the pitfalls of drugs and alcohol. Always remember that you can reach out for help from a friend, a trusted adult or teacher, or a guidance counselor when you need it.

You may think you are helping a loved one by throwing away hidden drugs or alcohol, but a person won't get help until he or she is ready.

CHAPTER 4

When and How You Can Help

*R*ich looked at his older brother passed out on the couch. Moving closer, Rich could smell the alcohol as his brother exhaled. Rich felt disgusted with him.

Then Rich remembered how his parents constantly reminded his brother to set a good example. Get good grades, be respectful, go out for sports, don't be late to work, show Rich the "right way to act." Rich started thinking, maybe his brother drank because of all this pressure. Suddenly Rich felt guilty. Could he be responsible for his brother's substance abuse? Should he be doing more to help him?

Rich went to where his parents kept the liquor. Collecting all the bottles, he started pouring their contents down the drain. When he finished, Rich searched his brother's room, car, and other hiding *places. Rich dumped any alcoholic beverage he could find. Relieved, Rich fell into the easy chair and thought, Wow, I finally helped him. Without any alcohol, he is sure to sober up.*

Rich believed that once his brother was sober, he could explain to him how his drinking problem was hurting his family and friends. He would tell his brother the effect drinking was having on his health and future. Rich believed he could help his brother by keeping him sober and relying on his brother's better judgment.

Rich thought he was helping, but actually he wasn't. His brother would just buy, share, or possibly steal more alcohol once his body craved the chemical substance. Like Rich, you want to help your loved one. But before you can do that, you must learn what it means to help. Sometimes it means letting go.

In the previous chapter you read how covering up for your loved one enables him or her to maintain the addiction. You must allow your loved one to face the consequences of his or her actions. By letting this happen, you will help. In a sense, to start assisting your loved one toward recovery, you must find the right ways to help.

All the good intentions you have will not convince your loved one to give up the substance abuse. Your loved one needs to recognize and understand the consequences of the addiction on his or her own. Your loved one can't begin to see the consequences until you let him or her suffer the consequences. He or she will not even consider getting or accepting help until he or she realizes there is a problem.

After what you have just read, you may feel your situation is hopeless. But that is not true. In fact, you have already started helping your loved one just by reading this book. That is because the first way to help is to learn about addiction. Reading books on addiction and recovery and learning how addiction happens help you understand your loved one. Learning a healthier way to react to a loved one's substance abuse may help the person to accept the problem sooner. By educating yourself on what your loved one will face when he or she is willing to accept help, you can prepare to provide the right support.

Tough Love

A block from home, Jamie noticed the flashing lights. Police, she thought. Now what had her sister done! Jamie remembered all the times her sister and her sister's friends had trashed the house while they were high. Each time, Jamie's parents had accepted responsibility for her sister's actions. They paid the fines, apologized to the neighbors, cleaned up the mess, and promised their daughter wouldn't cause any more trouble.

This time was different. As Jamie ran past the car and into the house, she noticed her sister was handcuffed and sitting in the backseat of the police car. She saw her parents talking to the police officers. Both of her parents were shaking their heads. The police officers walked outside, got into their car, and drove off. Jamie was shocked; her sister was on her way to jail.

Jamie's parents are helping her sister. This time, they are not covering up for their daughter. They are forcing her to face the consequences of her addiction. Jamie's sister may feel as if her parents have abandoned her. She may be thinking that they hate her. After all, if they cared, would they send her to jail? But none of this is true. Jamie's parents are loving and caring. They know their actions may alienate their daughter, but they also believe that this is the only way to help her. Jamie's parents are practicing Tough Love.

Tough Love is a program that can help a loved one who is addicted. This method can benefit a friend or sibling. Practicing Tough Love forces someone who is a substance abuser to become accountable for his or her actions. Tough Love is also used as a way to keep a loved one from getting into more serious trouble with the law. In most cases, Tough Love is used to force the addicted person into a rehabilitation program.

Persons under eighteen years of age usually live at home. Because of their age, a parent or guardian has the legal right to sign them into a rehabilitation program. Tough Love depends on this ability to control and force the addicted person to follow specific behaviors. Therefore, it is most often used when the substance abuser is a minor. Without this control, some persons who are addicted may be unwilling to consider rehabilitation.

Your loved one may now be in rehabilitation, which is a positive step, but Tough Love does have its problems. Sometimes, parents who practice Tough Love can seem cruel and unloving. These impressions can cause your loved one to drift further away. It may appear that the situation has gotten worse. Also, keep in mind that the substance abuser may not be ready to accept help. If this is true, the addicted person may fake participation in the rehabilitation program. Remember, recovery cannot start until the person who is addicted wants to accept help.

Intervention

Beth was scared. Her mom looked terrible. She knew her mother abused drugs but had only recently noticed how sick her mom was becoming. Beth had known for a long time how her mom's addiction was affecting their family and their lives. She had tried several times to get her mother to recognize her addiction. But every time, her mom came up with another excuse and denied she was addicted. Now, looking at her mother's drawn, pale, and pained face, Beth felt she had to do something.

Beth called her aunt. After listening patiently, Aunt Sue told Beth it was time to force her mom to accept her situation and her addiction. It was time to try intervention. Together, she, Beth, other family members, some close friends, and a trained counselor would get help for Beth's mom.

Most drug-addicted people deny their addiction. Until these people believe that they are substance abusers, they will not accept help. Intervention is a method designed to make an addicted loved one face the consequences of his or her actions. It brings the addicted person out of denial.

Intervention is a process that begins by contacting a chemical-dependency treatment center and getting the help of a certified counselor. Together, the counselor, family, friends, and sometimes an employer make the required arrangements.

The intervention meeting requires weeks of preparation. Your loved one's friends, your family, and an employer, who cares for and values your loved one, participate in a training meeting. At this meeting the counselor explains how each person should behave during the intervention.

Participants are told to be supportive and loving, but they are told not to confront the addicted person. Confrontation will make your loved one defensive and make the problem worse.

Everyone is told to be ready to state problem behaviors they have experienced when dealing with the addicted person. Each participant makes it clear that they blame these behaviors on the chemical substances. Also, everyone must be prepared to state what they will do if the loved one does not accept treatment. Once everyone is ready, the intervention meeting is arranged.

At the time intervention is to occur, everyone involved arrives at the meeting location before the addicted person. The location can be the counselor's office, your loved one's home, or his or her place of business. When your loved one arrives, he or she will probably be very surprised and possibly angry. The meeting begins with the counselor telling your loved one that everyone present cares about him or her. The counselor asks the addicted person to please sit and listen to what everyone has to say. He or she is asked not to question anyone until everyone has finished speaking.

Once everything has been said, the addicted person starts to realize that the support system is crumbling. He or she now knows that no one will cover up or take responsibility for his or her actions. Your loved one must now face the consequences of the addiction alone, or admit to the problem and accept treatment. When the decision is made to accept treatment, the addicted person immediately enters the treatment center.

It is important to understand that intervention may not work the first time. All those involved in the intervention must keep their promise. They must not enable the addiction. If your loved one continues his or her addictive behavior, it is important that he or she loses the "support group." Then intervention can be tried again, and this time it may succeed.

Helping the person you love face and deal with addiction requires you to remain strong. It is important that you constantly remember

As your loved one recovers, he or she will need your patience and understanding.

that it is the chemical substance causing the problem behavior. And be aware that once help is accepted, your loved one will need all your love and support.

Help Yourself

Another way to help your loved one is to help yourself. You are currently dealing with unusual and difficult situations. Your emotions are in turmoil. You may feel alone and unhappy. You can improve your outlook and ease your stress by finding someone in whom you can confide. This may be one person or a support group (people involved in similar situations who meet and share their feelings and problems). Here are some suggestions:

- a trusted friend
- an extended family member, like an aunt, uncle, or grandparent
- a sibling
- a teacher
- a guidance counselor
- your religious leader
- a support group organized by your school
- a support group organized by your community or local hospital
- professional support groups, such as Alateen and Al-Anon.

Remember, you are not alone. Many people have siblings, friends, or parents who are substance abusers. Try not to feel ashamed, embarrassed, or responsible. You are not the reason your loved one is addicted. You are not at fault. Accepting that you are not to blame, facing your situation, and taking actions that will help you cope are important steps in helping yourself and your loved one.

CHAPTER 5

What the Future Holds

*P*hil wouldn't look back as he walked with his parents to the car. They had just admitted his sister to the hospital's drug detoxification program. Phil stared at the car floor as they started to pull out of the parking space. He felt relieved; a huge weight had been lifted and now he could relax. His sister was finally accepting help and would no longer embarrass or disappoint him.

But relief turned to guilt. He looked back toward the hospital and felt he was abandoning her when she needed him most.

You may have similar feelings if your loved one has entered a drug or alcohol treatment center. You have every right to feel relieved. Your loved one has taken a step that will affect all the lives of the people who care for him or her. Your loved one has started the recovery process.

The Recovery Process
Recovery is a three-step process. Your loved one will go through:

- Detoxification
- Rehabilitation
- Aftercare

Detoxification is a medical procedure that helps your loved one through withdrawal. Your loved one will be under medical care during this time. He or she may be assigned a trained counselor and a "buddy." A buddy is another patient who has already completed detoxification. These people provide your loved one with encouragement and support during this portion of the treatment. Detoxification may last between two and four days.

Rehabilitation provides a protected and controlled environment that allows your loved one time to accept his or her disease. This involves activities designed to modify the addicted person's lifestyle. A person recovering from addiction must follow a specified daily routine. These practices are designed to help the person develop a healthier way of life, learn self-discipline, and take responsibility for his or her well-being. Your loved one may spend up to thirty days in this phase of the recovery process.

Aftercare begins when the person leaves the treatment center and returns to his or her daily routine. Participation in support group meetings, which began while in treatment, is now part of the daily routine. Attending these support group meetings is essential for recovery.

During recovery your loved one may attend and follow a twelve-step program. Alcoholics Anonymous created the first twelve-step program. Now several exist. These programs help your loved one understand why he or she turned to drugs and alcohol, and that addiction is a disease. Your loved one will learn how to face problems without turning to drugs and how to avoid returning to his or her old way of life. The following organizations have twelve-step programs:

- Alcoholics Anonymous (AA)
- Narcotics Anonymous (NA)
- Cocaine Anonymous (CA)
- Al-Anon—support group for families of substance abusers
- Alateen—support group for teenagers in families of substance abusers

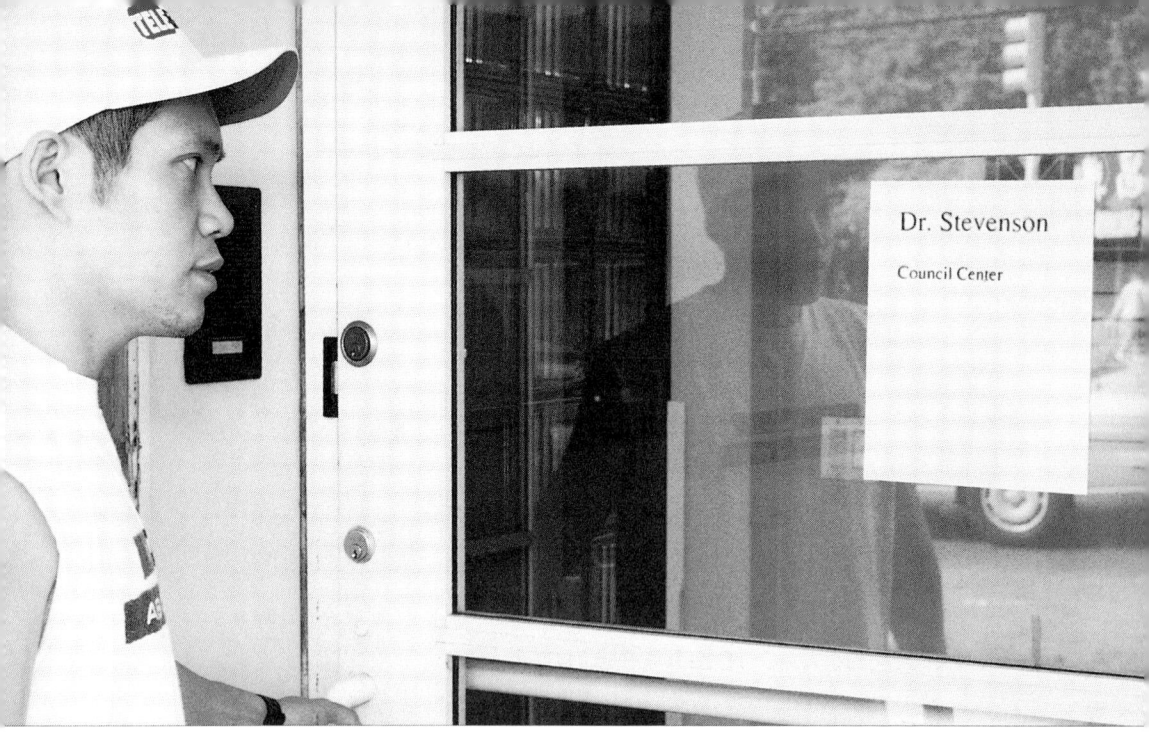

Your loved one will need physical and psychological care to recover from addiction. It is a lifelong process.

- Adult Children of Alcoholics—support group for adults whose parents abused alcohol
- National Association for Children of Alcoholics—support group for children of alcohol abusers

The Recovery Process and You

Phil answers the phone and hears his sister's voice. She's been in treatment for four days and he can't believe how good she sounds. She says she misses him and can't wait until he can visit.

Phil calls his mom to the phone. His mom looks thrilled as she begins to chat with his sister. Suddenly Phil hears his mom's voice become stern. Now he begins to listen to what his mom is telling his sister.

When his mom hangs up the phone, Phil yells, "Why can't she come home for a short visit? Didn't you hear how great she sounded? You must miss her, too! Why?"

Like Phil, you miss your loved one and are anxious for him or her to come home. But Phil's mom is doing the right thing. It is important that your loved one remain in treatment and follow all the rules.

While your loved one is in the treatment center, you and your family will have rules to follow too. These rules will limit how often and when you can visit. They will also limit telephone calls. You will be asked to support both your loved one and the recommendations of his or her counselor. As the recovery process progresses, you, your family, and friends may be asked to participate in your loved one's support group sessions.

While your loved one is in treatment, you and your family should seek help as well. There are support groups that help children, teens, and families understand what their loved one is feeling and experiencing. These support groups also help you and your family share your feelings, hopes, and fears.

Recovery can be a scary time for everyone, and no one should have to face the process alone. Always remember that you are not alone. Many people have friends, siblings, or parents who are suffering from addiction. A lot of these people attend support groups. The members of support groups do not judge, condemn, or criticize. Support group members share. It's important that you and your family get the help you deserve.

When Your Loved One Comes Home

Phil and his parents were bringing his sister home today. Everyone was happy and excited, except Phil. Phil felt nervous and scared. He loved his sister very much and wanted her to come home. But would she stay straight? What if she went back to her old habits?

Leaving the treatment center does not guarantee recovery. And it certainly can be difficult to adjust to new rules. But your loved one will need your support, help, love, and understanding. Your loved one may have to miss an important sporting event, dance recital, or award presentation to attend a support group meeting. In this situation, your loved one needs to know that you understand and support his or her choice. You must make it clear to your loved one that his or her successful recovery from addiction is important to you.

Sometimes you may see that someone is trying to tempt your loved one into using again. At these times you have to resist the urge to run out and help your loved one. You must let your loved one stand up for his or her new way of life. And when he or she does, tell them how proud he or she made you feel.

Your loved one has a long, hard journey ahead and needs you to be there for support. Patience, understanding, forgiveness, and love are essential.

Recovery or Relapse

Recovery is a lifelong process. Persons who abused drugs and alcohol need to learn that in order to control their disease they must never use alcohol or drugs again. Relapse can happen, and if it does, it will be painful for you. But every day your loved one is drug free, he or she becomes stronger.

Recovery takes patience and understanding. It requires your support and participation. You and your loved one must work together toward success. Remember, you and your loved one are not alone. There are a lot of people who have gone through the same or similar situations. They can help you and your loved one win the battle of addiction. Successful recovery is possible for your loved one.

Glossary

addiction An obsessive/compulsive need for and use of a substance or behavior.
alienate To make someone feel alone.
codependency A way a friend, sibling, or spouse of an addicted person behaves that unwillingly helps the person maintain his or her addiction.
detoxification The medical procedure used to aid chemically dependent persons through withdrawal.
intervention A process organized by family and friends to force an addicted person to admit to his or her addiction and enter a treatment center.
psychological Having to do with the mind.
rehabilitation A regulated and controlled treatment environment used to educate and retrain addicted persons.
relapse When an addicted person starts using drugs again after going through treatment.

susceptible More likely to happen.

tolerance When the body needs more and more of a drug to get the original effect.

Tough Love A practice parents or guardians can use to force a drug- or alcohol-addicted minor into a rehabilitation program.

withdrawal symptoms Painful physical problems that an addicted person experiences when he or she stops using drugs or alcohol.

Where to Go for Help

Al-Anon Family Group Headquarters, Inc.
1600 Corporate Landing Parkway
Virginia Beach, VA 23456
(800) 344-2666
(800) 563-1600
Web sites: http://www.alanon.alateen.org or
 http://www.alateen.org

The Children of Alcoholics Foundation
P.O. Box 4185
Grand Central Station
New York, NY 10115
(800) 359-2623

CoAnon Family Groups
P.O. Box 64742-66
Los Angeles, CA 90064
(310) 859-2206

Cocaine Anonymous (CA)
3740 Overland Avenue, Suite G
Los Angeles, CA 90034
(800) 773-9999
Web site: http://www.netwizards.net/ recovery/na

Co-Dependents Anonymous/CoDA-Teen
P.O. Box 33577
Phoenix, AZ 85067-3577

Nar-Anon Family Groups
P.O. Box 2562
Palos Verdes Peninsula, CA 90274
(310) 547-5800

Narcotics Anonymous (NA)
P.O. Box 9999
Van Nuys, CA 91409
(818) 780-3951

National Clearinghouse for Alcohol and Drug Information (NCADI)
P.O. Box 2345
Rockville, MD 20847-2345
(800) 729-6686
Web site: http://www.health.org

In Canada:
Alcoholics Anonymous (AA)
National Public Information Canada
P.O. Box 6433-Station J
Ottawa, ON M4P 1K5
(613) 722-1830
(800) 443-4525

Kids Help
439 University Avenue, Suite 300
Toronto, ON M5G 1Y8
(800) 668-6868
Web site: http://kidshelp.sympatico.ca/index.html

For Further Reading

Berger, Gilda. *Addiction.* New York: Franklin Watts, 1992.
——. *Alcoholism and the Family.* New York: Franklin Watts, 1993.
DeStefano, Susan. *Drugs in the Family.* New York: Twenty-First Century Books, 1991.
Gutman, Bill. *Harmful to Your Health.* New York: Twenty-First Century Books, 1996.
Lee, Mary Price, and Richard S. Lee. *Drugs and Codependency.* New York: Rosen Publishing Group, 1995.
Phillips, Lynn. *Life Issues: Drug Abuse.* New York: Marshall Cavendish, 1994.
Seixas, Judith, S. *Living with a Parent Who Takes Drugs.* New York: Greenwillow Books, 1989.
Shuker-Haines, Frances. *Everything You Need to Know About a Drug-Abusing Parent.* Rev. ed. New York: Rosen Publishing Group, 1996.
Trapani, Margi. *Inside a Support Group: Help for Teenage Children of Alcoholics.* New York: The Rosen Publishing Group, Inc., 1997.

Index

A
abuse, 35-36
addiction, 9, 13, 14, 43, 48, 57
   to behaviors, 10
   causes, 9-21, 39
   consequences of, 42-44, 48
   coping with, 7
   defined, 10
   effects, 7, 20, 22-31, 38, 39
   as illness, 20-21, 35, 53, 55
   recovery from, 21, 31, 42-43, 45, 52, 53
   stages of, 10-13
addictive personality, 15-17
aftercare, 53, 54
Al-Anon, 38, 50, 53
alcohol, 6, 10, 12-13, 17-20, 39, 42, 57
   effects, 27-28
   experimenting with, 10, 19
Alcoholics Anonymous, 53
anger, 7, 25

C
codependency, 7, 36-38
counselors, 46-47, 48, 50, 52, 55

D
denial, 22, 23
depression, 22, 25
detoxification, 52
drugs, 6, 10, 12-13, 57
   as an escape, 17-18
   experimenting with, 11
   hallucinogens, 28-29
   narcotics, 29
   stimulants, 29-30
   tranquilizers, 28
   withdrawal from, 22, 26

E
enabling, 37, 42, 48
exercise, 10

F
family, 6-7, 16, 33, 39, 50
friends, 6-7, 33, 35, 36, 39, 44, 50, 56

G
gambling, 10
guilt, 7, 22, 23

I
illness, 10
intervention, 7, 46-49
isolation, 22, 26

M
mental illness, 14
moods, changing, 33-34

N
Nar-Anon, 38
Narcotics Anonymous, 53
National Institute of Drug Abuse (NIDA), 14

P
parents, 7, 14, 16, 18, 34, 35, 56
peer pressure, 19
perfectionism, 18

R
rebellion, 19
recovery, 7, 52-57
rehabilitation, 45, 52
relapse, 57
responsibilities, added, 34-35, 38

S
self-blame, 7, 37-38, 50

shame, 7, 22, 23, 50
shopping, 10
stress, 16, 17, 33-34, 39, 49
support groups, 38, 49, 50, 53-56

T
teachers, 6-7, 18
tolerance, 13
Tough Love, 7, 43-45
treatment, 21, 31, 48, 52, 55
treatment centers, 53, 55, 56
twelve-step programs, 53-54

V
violence, 23, 25, 26

About the Author
Jessica Hanan works developing and writing multimedia technology curricula for the high school market. She lives in Freehold, New Jersey, with her two daughters.

Photo Credits
Cover photo by Brian T. Silak; pp. 2, 8, 12, 15, 20, 23, 25, 30, 34, 36, 40, 49, 54 by Brian T. Silak; p. 27 by Seth Dinnerman; p. 38 Ira Fox.